THE EYES OF CRIMINAL LAW

JUN-HYUNG PARK

Copyright © 2018 Jun-Hyung Park

All rights reserved.

ISBN-13:9781729499733

We are not bettering our reason, but we are creating a good world with our reason.

JUN-HYUNG PARK

CONTENTS

⟨ THE EYES OF CRIMINAL LAW ⟩

1   THE EYES OF CRIMINAL LAW   11

2   ROBBERY AND RAPE   21

3   ILLEGALITY   31

4   ERROR   37

5   MENTAL ILLNESS   51

6   MINORS   61

7   REDUCTION   65

〈 Errors in the Conceptualization of the "Criminal Act" Based on the Principle of Essential Intent 〉

I INTRODUCTION   73

II CRIMES OF ROBBERY AND RAPE   78

III ERRORS CAUSED BY CRIMINAL
     INTENT IN THE CRIMES OF   85
     ROBBERY AND RAPE

IV SOLUTION   89

V CONCLUSION   99

This book does not consider god's law.
The expression of god's criminal law does not refer to god's law.

THE EYES OF CRIMINAL LAW

1. THE EYES OF CRIMINAL LAW

Maximized human reason pursued by modern people is eventually placed side by side with that of God. The eyes of criminal law have become God's eyes.

Criminal law charges crime. Charging crime refers to revealing crime and implementing punishment.

People created criminal law, and it is people who judge actions based on it. Thus, the eyes of criminal law that look upon crime are ultimately the eyes of the people. Regardless of who it is, or whether it is one person or a group of people, the eyes of criminal law always belong to the people.

The subject in the eyes of criminal law is important regardless of who the person is. This is because the subject decides what criminal law should be.

That the eyes of criminal law are the people's eyes means that before speaking of criminal law, we must seriously consider the existence of people.

Who are we? What is our existence? How must we live? Such questions are the beginning of criminal law. Criminal law is our philosophy and life.

Because the eyes of the criminal law are people's eyes, it is a matter of course that criminal law should be written from the viewpoint of the people.

Criminal law requires human judgment according to the written text, but if criminal law does not have people's eyes, it will not stop even where people feel uncomfortable and awkward. This will make us doubt whether it is the correct criminal law, and its persuasiveness will weaken, causing many problems. Unfortunately, most criminal laws do not have people's eyes.

To know whose eyes the criminal law has, we must look at intent in the criminal code. In most of the criminal law that we use, for a crime to exist, there must be intent.

Intent means doing something on purpose while being aware. In criminal law, criminal intent means intent. If we think about intent only within the scope of criminal law, we can refer to it as criminal intent—thus, the intent to commit.

There is no need to give a special meaning to intent applicable only to criminal law. The less a difference between terms used in law and terms used in everyday life, the better. This is more the case in criminal law, where terms must be concise, plain, and easy to understand. The concept of intent used in criminal law does not need to be different from the concept of intent used in everyday life, and this should be the case.

Intent is a person's innermost feelings, and it is impossible for other people to confirm this.

For example, if I have caused someone to be in a fraught situation without meaning to, I will tell that person that it was not my intent. Then, the other person may say or think that I did it intentionally or unintentionally. However, they cannot confirm if I had or did not have intent, though they may believe they can. Furthermore, I may be faced with a confusing situation where my mind is not clear, and even I cannot know my own thoughts or actions. That is nature of the human mind.

In any society, criminal law has an invaluable role. Criminal law must not only reveal crimes and impose punishment after a conviction of a crime but also regulate society and maintain it in a stable manner. Protecting or reforming a criminal is also in the interest of society. Thus, if required socially, a conclusion must be made although there may be parts that are somewhat ambiguous and beyond our control.

Though we may not know a person's innermost feelings,

if intent is required for a crime to exist due to realistic needs, it may be the only path that we can take.

Revealing the absolute truth goes beyond a person's ability. If we need only a consensus of the members of society regarding the absolute truth, we must accept that this is the best we can do.

Then, we must ask whether intent is required in criminal law. In much of the criminal code, intent is a prerequisite for a crime to exist. In the basic form, a crime is committed if someone consciously and deliberately commits an act. Only in certain designated cases can an act be a crime if someone commits the act without intent; hence, without intent, there is no crime. There is also criminal law that stipulates that if there is no intent, no punishment is imposed.

Some criminal law requires that intent must be present for a crime to exist for certain. However, let us think about the text that states that there is no punishment if there is no intent. We can interpret this as meaning that there is no crime and that, of course, punishment cannot be imposed. We can also think about a case where there is a crime but where no punishment is imposed.

What needs to be made clear here is that criminal law allows for the charge of a crime, which means that it reveals crimes and punishes. Thus, the words and sentences used in criminal law must be as concise and clear as possible, and they must be easy to understand so that anyone can interpret them. Criminal law must not use unnecessary modifiers, and if possible, it must be designed so that only one interpretation is possible.

If the criminal law states that intent is required for there to be a crime, there must be no crime when there is no intent. Then, the law should state that if there is no intent, there is no crime—not that there is no punishment, such that other unnecessary interpretations do not arise.

Intent in criminal law refers to criminal intent, and the criminal law that we use states that intent is required for a crime to exist. This cannot convince us. It was designed incorrectly from the beginning. This is because people cannot know others' innermost feelings.

For a person to reveal another person's crime, the criminal act or criminal situation must be revealed, not the criminal intent. This is how a crime is revealed.

The concept of intent is required in criminal law, but it is not required for there to be a crime as stated in the current criminal law. The intent referred to in criminal law must have the same concept of intent of which that most people think. Such "intent" is not required for there to be a crime, but it is used to determine the degree of punishment imposed.

The criminal law we use today was created based on modern thought. Modern people have emphasized human reason to overcome medieval theology. However, they were still thinking in a theological way, and they have had to overcome theology in order to become increase ling more obsessed with reason. They were unable to view people's reason as the reason that they as living and breathing people possessed, but they wanted instead to separate people from reason and give another meaning to reason itself. Maximized human reason pursued by modern people is eventually placed side by side with God. The eyes of criminal law have become God's eyes.

Modern people did not recognize people's reason as it was but rather sought an ideal state. We all dream of an ideal world. However, we cannot say that our reason and abilities must reach an ideal state that someone is seeking.

We are not bettering our reason but creating a good world with the reason we possess.

This is not an attempt to criticize modern people. Their achievements speak for themselves, and it is because of them that we exist today. Criminal law with the eyes of God was a limitation of not modern people but their best efforts.

It is inevitable that maximized reason—in other words, criminal law written with the eyes of God—would have God's perspective. Criminal law is made by the people and for the people, but it did not have the people's perspective. Thus, criminal law was designed incorrectly.

Criminal law in the eyes of God causes numerous problems. In particular, it may feel as if those making judgments based on criminal law have become God. It is inevitable that these judges feel this way. In addition, it will suffer from a gap between the law and reality.

If people were to judge based on criminal law with God's eyes, this is not a correct perspective, and it lacks persuasiveness. In other words, God's criminal law is not understandable.

Previously, we asked whether God's eyes are required for criminal law. It is time to answer this question. When an accusation of a crime is raised in accordance with criminal law, judges do not decide based on the intent of the person who committed the crime. Rather, their judgment is based on the objective situation, evidence, and logic. In such a judgment, there is no need to include a person's innermost feelings to make a legal judgment. Intent is used to control the level of punishment by considering the extent of punishment for criminals.

Imposing the appropriate amount of punishment is just as important as accurately revealing a crime. God's criminal law has the premise that crime can be unambiguously revealed, and there is a lack of concern about how much punishment should be given.

God's criminal law tries to rely on what is written in the law in imposing punishment. Compared with judging a crime, the extent of punishment to impose should rely more on a person's judgment than on what is written in the law.

Intent is not required for judging a crime based on criminal law, but it must affect how much punishment should be imposed. In criminal law, the problem is not whether intent exists but what the intent is.

Criminal law that states that intent is required for there to be a crime is criminal law with the eyes of God and is therefore problematic. I would like to state seriously what kind of criminal law we should use in this age. Let us put people's eyes on criminal law. It is now our turn.

2. ROBBERY AND RAPE

We cannot know someone's innermost feelings. Thus, in criminal law, intent is not required for a crime to exist, but it must be involved when imposing punishment.

Robbery and rape refer to a robber who commits rape. The point is to impose the greatest punishment of a robber who commits rape.

In robbery and rape, the two must have a close relationship, where the robber takes advantage of the victim's condition after the act of robbery and commits rape. Otherwise, the robbery and rape are separate crimes.

We must first consider whether to handle robbery and rape under the crime of robbery crime or the crime of rape.

In criminal law, in some cases, the crime of robbery and rape is defined under robbery and, in some cases, rape. Defining it under robbery is appropriate for the crime of robbery and rape.

Robbery is the base crime, and if rape is committed in addition, more severe punishment is imposed. Hence, punishment is more severe when robbery and rape are committed together than when robbery or rape is committed separately. The same structure applies to the crimes of robbery and murder. It is also valid for the crimes of robbery and murder to be determined under robbery instead of murder.

Robbery and rape or robbery and murder must be handled under robbery rather than rape or murder, as in many cases, when robbery is committed, other crimes are committed with it. In addition, rape or murder are worse crimes than robbery.

However, this does not mean that punishment for rape or murder must always be greater than that for robbery. These are emotional issues in our society. We think that rape is worse than robbery and that murder is worse than rape.

After defining various crimes, including murder, rape, and robbery, when creating criminal law, we felt a need to punish murder or rape more severely, as these crimes violate a person's life or sexual freedom, which is important. Thus, when robbery is committed together with rape or murder, the punishment must be more severe than when such crimes are committed separately.

At this point, there is the question as to the difference between robbery and rape and between rape and robbery. Let us return to the basic principle of criminal law.

Most criminal laws state that intent must be present for

a crime to exist. Intent cannot be defined precisely. Each criminal law may express it a little differently. However, in any criminal law, if intent is required for there to be a crime, if it is referred to as criminal intent or a criminal situation as the intent to commit, it will not be much different from the concept of the society in which the criminal law belongs.

Thus, in combination, robbery and rape represent a crime committed with close proximity between robbery and rape separately, and thus, there must be intent to rob and rape. Under the basic principle of criminal law that states that intent is required, in regard to robbery and rape, if there is the intent to rob and rape, it is sufficient, and the order of the robbery and rape is meaningless. Furthermore, there is no need to think about rape while committing robbery. It is sufficient if there is criminal intent for robbery or recognition of a rape situation.

Let us consider that under any criminal law, the combination of robbery and rape refers to a case in which the crime of robbery is committed first and then the rape is committed afterward because the intent toward rape arises, not in cases in which the intent to rob occurs after the rape is committed first and then robbery is committed.

Of course, if there is the criminal thought to commit both robbery and rape from the beginning, it is robbery and rape regardless of the order in which the crimes were committed. However, if even in this case, the crime and punishment that follows should be evaluated based on the order in which the robbery and rape were committed, which is a violation of a significant principle of criminal law that undermines the equity of punishment.

Let us consider the reason for approaching the robbery and rape crime differently based on the order in which the two crimes were committed. This is a strong warning against robbers who are attempting to commit rape, since the robber will receive a harsher punishment if he/she also commits rape. It also means that rape is a worse crime than robbery.

At first glance, this may seem correct, but this should not be overlooked. This is a question of whether we should implement deterrence measures for someone attempting to commit rape after committing robbery.

Of course, if someone commits robbery and rape together, they will receive a harsher punishment than if they committed only a robbery even if a separate crime of robbery and rape does not exist in criminal law. Thus, there is no absence of punishment.

It is important, therefore, to look at the deterrent for the crime of robbery and rape by focusing on the degree of punishment—that is, punishing more heavily when the two crimes are committed together than when they are committed separately. Only then can the objective of criminal law to punish robbery and rape more severely be achieved.

First, let us think of a case in which the person who has committed robbery gives up before they commit rape because they are afraid of the severe punishment for robbery and rape. In this case, it can be said that the objective of the legislation was correct.

However, we can also think of another case. Let us think of a case in which it is revealed that a person who intends to commit robbery and rape intentionally commits rape first and then commits robbery. What if this person planned to make a false claim that they committed the crime of rape and the crime of robbery instead of robbery and rape? If this false claim is accepted, the cunning criminal will receive a lighter punishment than intended.

This is a real problem. If a person who judges a crime pursuant to the criminal code considers the circumstances of the crime and judges that the criminal had the intent to commit robbery and rape from the beginning or the criminal committed the rape after the robbery; the crime then becomes a crime of robbery and rape. However, if it is judged that the criminal committed a robbery after the rape, it is not a crime of robbery and rape. Then, the problem is what punishment the criminal should receive rather than what crime occurred.

Imposing punishment is as important as revealing a crime. It is a matter of course to reveal whether robbery or rape was committed. However, deciding whether it was a robbery and rape or a rape and robbery is a different matter.

The criterion for deciding whether it was robbery and rape or a rape and robbery should not concern the order in which the crimes were committed but concern the intent of the criminal. However, we cannot know the criminal's innermost feelings. We cannot know someone's innermost feelings. Thus, in criminal law, intent is not required for a crime to exist, but it must be involved when imposing punishment.

There is no problem without distinguishing whether the crime of robbery and rape was committed when a robber committed rape or when a rapist committed robbery. However, if it is distinguished, it raises the question of the equitable nature of punishment and the problem of lighter punishment for sly criminals.

If criminal law has the eyes of God, it is a matter of course that the crime of the person who intended to commit robbery and rape from the beginning was robbery and rape regardless of the order in which the crimes were committed. It would also be robbery and rape even if the rape was committed after the intent to the rape arose after the robbery.

Of course, for it to be a crime of robbery and rape, the robbery and rape must be closely related. Otherwise, the robbery and rape will be established separately, and the punishment will not be as heavy as for the crime of robbery and rape.

However, it is not robbery and rape if the robbery was committed after the intent to rob arose after the rape.

Under criminal law with the people's eyes, regarding the crime of rape and robbery, there is no need to differentiate the crime of robbery and rape and rape and robbery based on the intent of the criminal, which cannot be known. Of course, robbery and rape must be closely linked, but the order does not matter.

The intent to rob and rape will relate to the degree of punishment for the criminal.

I would like to stress that under the people's criminal law, the crime of robbery and rape should be discussed not in terms of what kind of crime it is but in terms of what punishment the criminal should receive.

3. ILLEGALITY

Because the law governs our life, we must do our best to ensure that all members of society can access it. This is more the case for criminal law, as it deals with crimes.

Let us consider what responses would be provided when someone who is unfamiliar with the terms used in criminology is asked about the difference between illegality in criminal law and unlawfulness. They will probably say that they are similar. That is the correct answer. Illegality and unlawfulness have similar meanings.

Criminal law should be written so that anyone can understand it, and it would not be beneficial if illegality in criminal law were to have special meaning that goes beyond the way it is generally used.

If necessary, a new meaning can be given to a word that is widely used. However, we must consider whether this is truly required.

In many criminal laws, illegality and unlawfulness are given different meanings. I do not understand this difference. Perhaps unlawfulness is something that people can think of more easily, meaning something that is against the law, while illegality is the step prior to unlawfulness. Thus, something is illegal first and then unlawful.

Let us look at an example. Let us suppose that someone has killed a person. This person's act is illegal. However, if that person committed murder in self-defense, the illegality is shattered, and the act is not a crime. This person committed murder illegally, but if it was in self-defense, the illegality is shattered, and it is therefore not unlawful. This sounds plausible. However, it feels awkward and complicated. There are varied and complicated arguments with regard to the concept of illegality.

Usually, criminal law, which includes the concept of illegality, states that self-defense for unjust infringement shatters illegality, and the act is not punished or is not considered a crime.

In this case, it is correct to say that the act is not a crime. This is because self-defense is just, and the act thus cannot be a crime and cannot therefore be punished. Thus, in criminal law, self-defense is not a crime.

Criminal law includes the crime of murder, which stipulates that if one kills a person, it is a crime. On the other hand, there is self-defense, which stipulates that just defense is not a crime. Thus, when a person is killed in self-defense, the self-defense written in criminal law applies immediately, and the act does not become a crime.

It may be added that self-defense is excluded for murder; hence, people will not misunderstand. If this is the case, such exceptions will have to be included repetitively for all crimes. This will make things more complicated and inconvenient. Thus, such self-defense is not a crime, which is written separately and applied generally.

The example of self-defense that we are looking at now is special. Justly defending oneself is necessary for our survival. Even if self-defense is not written in criminal law, just defense is not a crime.

Before self-defense is observed under criminal law, it is a question of our survival and instincts. We do whatever it takes to protect ourselves and to survive. If it does not violate the sentiments of our society, it is, of course, not a crime.

This applies to anything else that shatters illegality. Let us look at justifiable acts. A justifiable act is not a crime. Under many criminal laws, if a just act corresponds to a crime written in the criminal law, it is first illegal. Afterward, if it is a just act, the illegality is shattered, and the act is not a crime or is not punished.

The fact that the act is first illegal is wrong. As explained previously, the act is not a crime because it is a just act, not because it is illegal at first but because the illegality is shattered.

What is the reason for stating that something is illegal though it is not a crime and then shattering the illegality? It is for academic amusement. It is more amusing to state that something is illegal but that it is not a crime because there are reasons that shatter the illegality rather than simply stating that it is not a crime. This also shows the way in which modern people think.

It is not wrong to enjoy a little amusement in academics. It can increase interest and enrich the discipline. However, one must refrain from academics in the field of the law.

Because the law governs our life, we must do our best to ensure that all members of society can access it. This is more so the case for criminal law, as it deals with crimes.

Through the introduction of the concept of illegality in criminal law and through increasing the number of steps in the process of imposing crimes, numerous arguments have emerged. Such arguments plant negative impressions of criminal law, making people feel that criminal law is difficult, complicated, and based on in-depth theories and therefore difficult to understand.

There is no reason to distinguish illegality and unlawfulness, which means that there is no need to give special meaning to illegality in criminal law. If possible, criminal law should be concise, simple, and clear.

Let us get rid of the concept that illegality has a special meaning in criminal law.

4. ERROR

God's criminal law takes unrealistic assumptions as given. It does not see the object of criminal law, as it is and moves away from the truth by widening the scope of error in going through each step.

Error was always our main concern. It was the object of research of many scholars, and it is especially of interest in the field of psychology.

In existing law, error is mostly about the type of error and the solution. Whereas in psychology, we examine why people make mistakes and in which psychological state mistakes occur, as well as the cause of such errors.

Let us think about how criminal law should address errors. God's criminal law is concerned only with the number of cases. It is not interested in why people make errors and what it means. It is as if a non-human entity has been classified based on outer appearance without understanding human error.

In criminal law, errors should be approached from the perspective of the people, not from the perspective of God. That is because those who judge based on criminal law are people.

Furthermore, the perspective with which one approaches oneself is not appropriate as the perspective of criminal law. Exploring the existence of people based on one's own reason and based on oneself is a good way to practice philosophy, but it cannot be said that this applies as a way of enforcing criminal law. This is because the eyes of criminal law are the eyes of other people looking upon someone else.

If there is a philosophical outcome, this can be material in applying criminal law, but the philosophical outcome itself does not always apply to criminal law. In particular, if one is overwhelmed by famous scholars and well-known theories, one does not have the right attitude for research.

It has been said that the field of psychology is interested in why people make errors. This is because the reason for the error is important, not the type of error. This is also the case for criminal law.

If a person who commits a crime argues that there was an error or if there was reason to believe so, we must put the reason for that error on the table and consider its validity. At the end of the deliberation, we must reach the conclusion of what punishment should be given to the criminal.

However, our current criminal law does not do this. At the end of deliberating on the criminal's error, we judge whether the person committed a crime.

Let us look at an example. Let us suppose that someone has committed murder. This person argues that while hunting with a friend at night, he accidentally shot his friend after mistaking him for a deer.

In this case, under both God's or people's criminal law, we must seek to find the truth by observing the circumstances of the error. However, the conclusion of the deliberation is different under the different laws.

When the certain judgment of a murder is reached and what remains is the issue of the error, at the end of the deliberation, God's law judges whether a crime has been committed. However, under the people's criminal law, the act is definitely a crime, and at the end of the deliberation, we must decide whether to punish the criminal and, if so, how severe the punishment must be.

According to God's law, if the murder occurred because the friend was mistaken for a deer, this means that there was no intent, and therefore there was no crime, and we can speculate that the crime occurred due to neglect.

The murderer may have fired the gun thinking that their friend was a deer out of a misunderstanding. However, the murderer might be lying about the error.

I do not doubt the efforts of people trying to reveal the truth. It is somewhat reasonable to argue that if the person who shot and killed their friend thought that they were shooting a deer; the act (shooting a person) that goes beyond their awareness (shooting a deer) is not a crime.

However, let us think further. A person is just a person. Even if someone thought that a person was a deer, that person does not become a deer.

Someone is the murderer, and someone is the murder victim. When the murder victim has no voice and when the murderer argues that it was an error, criminal law does not necessarily have to judge whether there was a crime. If there is an absolute need to do so, it must be done. However, we can choose to take a more accurate and rational road.

According to the people's criminal law, if it is certain that a person was killed, then, of course, there is a murder, and if the criminal argues that he mistook his friend for a deer and if there is reason to believe so, this can be considered in deciding which punishment at which severity level to give.

As mentioned previously, we cannot know someone's innermost feelings about their intent, and such intent is not necessary for there to be a crime, but it is necessary for deciding about the punishment. The same applies to the errors.

If someone has committed a crime, we cannot know for certain if that person committed a crime due to an error.

Let us think of a case in which the criminal does not state the truth. He may state that he made an error when he did not or that he did not make an error when he did. However, that will inevitably become the criminal's argument.

Let us suppose that such an argument or the circumstances are persuasive enough that the person determining the crime accepts the argument. Then, we should decide whether there is a crime? This is an attempt to decide whether an error can be a crime.

Under God's criminal law, which states that intent is required for there to be a crime, in the case of an error, there is of course no intent, and therefore, the act is not a crime. As explained previously, it must be stated that there is no crime instead of not conducting sentencing.

Under the people's criminal law, where intent is involved in deciding on the degree of punishment to sentence, the criminal's argument that he made an error is not a matter of whether there is a crime; rather, it is a matter of the degree of punishment.

We looked at illegality in the previous chapter. Criminal law, which introduces the concept of illegality, increases the number of steps required in imposing a crime and has caused many unnecessary claims.

If under God's criminal law, error prevents an act from becoming a crime, criminal law becomes even more complicated. If the number of errors is added to each step in determining a crime, there are various abstruse theories about how to judge, what crime it becomes, and how much punishment to give when it comes to each case.

This has complicated criminal law, which should be

concise, and it has turned into a difficult language that must be studied to be comprehended, though criminal law should be understood by anyone.

If the existence of various theories in criminal law is regarded as a principle, this can be positively viewed because it diversifies and enriches the field. However, if unconvincing theories that cannot be understood dominate criminal law and exist within it, this is unfortunate for the members of society using this law.

Let us look at an example according to God's criminal law. Let us add error to self-defense, which we looked at previously. A soldier in the battlefield claims to have pulled the trigger to make his fellow soldiers laugh, thinking that the gun was unloaded. In fact, it was a loaded gun, and the fellow soldier who had been shot, died. However, the dead fellow soldier had his finger on his gun's trigger. It was revealed that he had harbored a grudge against the shooter for a while, and he did so for the right when he was about to shoot him, when he was shot and killed first.

The shooter's situation may seem like self-defense. However, the shooter pulled the trigger to play a prank and was not thinking about self-defense. Self-defense is a way to shatter the steps of illegality, but self-defense was not recognized in this situation, and the fellow soldier was killed due to an error.

Those who side with God's criminal law like to raise this example. They highly value solving a problem by combining various theories when there are numerous complex cases in accordance with each step and situation.

This is for academic amusement. The example presented previously is quite strange and very unlikely to happen in real life. However, let us suppose that such a series of events occurred. In fact, let us suppose that the person making a judgment based on criminal law judges that such a situation occurred. Let us think of what would happen if this judge determined that the error argument was false.

In the case of the people's criminal law, the conclusion is the same. We know that recognizing self-defense is the best we can do.

Let us suppose that we have recognized self-defense. In this case, the criminal may state that he was aware because he knew of the situation surrounding self-defense or that he was not aware although he did know. Alternatively, he could state that he did not know because he did not or that he knew even though he did not.

Regardless of what the criminal's claim is, if the person determining the crime recognizes the situation surrounding self-defense, it is wise not to recognize the crime regardless of whether there was awareness of the situation. Because there is a situation in which there is no crime, this overpowers the assumption of crime.

Such an argument is quite awkward. That is because the situation proposed earlier is unlikely to happen. Thus, judging a God's criminal case situation with the people's criminal law is not very significant.

The assumption that the self-defense situation is certain is also awkward. That is because whether the self-defense situation is correct must be fiercely weighed and deliberated in the process of making a judgment according to criminal law.

God's criminal law assumes self-defense, but the people's criminal law deliberates self-defense.

God's criminal law takes unrealistic assumptions as

given. It does not see the object of the criminal law, as it is and moves away from the truth by widening the scope of error as it goes through each step.

A crime committed because of an error means that the crime was committed without intent, and therefore, under God's criminal law, it is not a crime. When punishment is to be given, punishment is given exceptionally, as it is a crime of error.

Under the people's criminal law, the question is not whether the error is a crime or not, but the question is how much punishment to give.

What is interesting here is that most criminal law is strict not about the error in the circumstances of the crime but when it is stated that it was unknown that the act would be considered a crime.

If a criminal law states that intent is required for there to be a crime, it is correct to think that the act is a crime, as the act was committed even though it was known that the actor himself knew that he would be committing a crime rather than simply knowing about the situation of the crime. Then, even if he knew about the situation of the crime but did not know that the act would be a crime, there is no intent. Thus, it is not considered a crime, and all that is left is whether to treat it as an error.

There is a practicality in the reason for most criminal laws being strict in the above situation. Criminal situations are proved based on evidence or testimonies, but anyone can state that they did not know that it would be a crime.

The criminal is bound to make excuses, and if they do, it means that by narrowing the scope of recognition of error, it is basically a crime with intention, but if the criminal is particularly persuasive, their act will not become a crime. There is also a criminal law that leaves room to decrease punishment even if the crime is acknowledged.

This is not in line with God's criminal law. There are many points like this in criminal law, though God's criminal law states that if there is intent, there is crime, and if there is not, it is not, so determining intent is impossible. Thus, content that is incompatible with God's criminal law exists throughout the law.

This does not mean that the principles of criminal law should be destroyed. It is a device based on real needs to prevent the criminal law with the eyes of God from being out of balance and collapsing on its own.

5. MENTAL ILLNESS

God's criminal law assumes that people's reason is the same as God's and that it explains how crimes should be addressed. God's criminal law should explain why a person can become God before speaking of crime and punishment.

If mental illness exists, there is no intent in God's criminal law. If there is no intent, of course, there is no crime.

There are many criminal laws that state that an act is not a crime in the case of severe mental illness and mete out weaker punishment in the case of slight mental illness. Thus, many criminal laws stipulate that there is no intent in the case of severe mental illness and that there is error in the case of slight mental illness.

If there is mental illness, they may be no intent and therefore no crime. This refers to God's criminal law. Under the people's criminal law, with regard to mental illness, though a crime is recognized, either punishment is not given or it is lessened.

Modern people accurately reveal the degree of mental illness of the criminal law in question, and if the degree is severe enough to obstruct intent, then they do not wish to turn the patient into a criminal, which is respectful.

However, this is impossible. It may be very difficult and awkward to recognize that this is impossible. When all these factors are considered, we may feel that accepting and maintaining God's criminal law is the best method. We may also feel that not deeming the act committed by a patient is a crime is more appropriate for protecting the patient than giving no punishment or less punishment. However, we cannot say that the criminal's act is not a crime in an effort to be considerate of a criminal.

There are various causes of mental illness. Some people may have been born with physical disabilities, or others may have developed mental illnesses due to other illnesses that occur in certain situations.

The most problematic argument is the one stating that consciousness was lost due to drugs or alcohol. Accepting the criminal's argument that they have no recollection because they were drunk and giving them a lesser punishment is, in most cases, contradictory to what members of society can accept and is becoming a social issue.

Let us think of two situations. In the first situation, a person on drugs injured a passerby on the street by hitting them with a blunt object for no reason. In the second situation, a person on drugs injured a passerby on the street by hitting them with a blunt object while they were unconscious.

In this situation, according to God's criminal law, if the degree to which the attacker was affected by the drugs was sufficient enough to establish that the attacker had no judgment or volition, there is no intent and therefore no crime. What is important here is the degree to which the attacker was affected by drugs and whether the attacker was conscious while swinging the blunt object.

Two situations were laid out previously. The first involves an objective situation. In the second, it was determined that the criminal had been high on drugs and already lost their consciousness. Those who follow God's criminal law like to bring up examples such as the second situation.

The most important part is whether the criminal who committed the attack had taken drugs and was unconscious from the effect of the drugs when the crime was committed or whether the criminal was falsely claiming such that the potential criminal lost his/her consciousness to avoid punishment. This part will without a doubt be the most important point in making a judgment based on criminal law. This is because people cannot know other people's innermost feelings.

Furthermore, in many cases, the criminal claims are that they do not remember anything. The criminal's state of mind during the crime is what is important. That the criminal does not remember what happened afterward does not determine whether the act was a crime.

To avoid such perplexing situations (judgment on the degree of mental illness will determine whether there was a crime because under Gods' criminal law, there must be intent for there to be a crime), those who follow God's criminal law propose a situation in which the criminal's degree of mental illness is already determined and thus explain what must be done in the situation in question. This way of thinking occurs in all areas related to intent.

To give another example, when explaining self-defense, whether we can acknowledge self-defense as a key point, but under God's criminal law, whether it is self-defense and whether it considered under certain circumstances is already determined before the punishment that should be administered.

People cannot become God. God's criminal law assumes

that people's reason is the same as God's and explains how crimes should be addressed. It clearly amuses that God imagine dealing with crime. However, criminal law is not for amusement. It exists to deliberate on crimes. God's criminal law should explain why a person can become God before speaking of crime and punishment.

How would a judge determining crime based on criminal law think when someone claims mental illness? According to God's criminal law, if it is determined that the criminal lost consciousness because of drugs and lost control, it would have to be determined that there was no crime. If not, it will be a crime.

According to people's criminal law, before considering the argument that the criminal was high on drugs, it must be determined whether the criminal really injured a passerby by hitting them with a blunt object. If this is deemed true, the crime of injuring a person must be acknowledged first, and the criminal's claim about mental illness must then be considered before the degree of punishment is determined.

God's criminal law and the people's criminal law both determine whether the crime was committed by the criminal while they were unconscious. However, the results are different. There is a definite differences between acknowledging mental illness in the step where the existence of the crime is being determined and acknowledging mental illness in the step where the punishment is assigned to the criminal.

Giving a criminal the appropriate punishment is as important as revealing the crime under criminal law. We determine the existence of a crime and mete punishment under criminal law. In doing so, we use everything at our disposal to draw the best conclusion, not to confirm whether the criminal was mentally ill.

Of course, it can be determined legally whether there was mental illness; but whether there is no need to do so, it is better not to do. The person making a legal conclusion is just a person. It is painful for a person to do something that people cannot. It is worse for people whose jobs are determining the existence of crimes.

Then, we have no reason to determine whether crime exists with a person's mental state, which cannot be accurately confirmed. Mental illness should be considered in the punishment step and in determining whether the criminal requires treatment. However, this does not mean that mental illness has been accurately confirmed.

Some criminal laws state that if the criminal induces a state of unconsciousness themselves by consuming alcohol or drugs before committing the crime, they will be punished even if their mind was not sound while committing the crime.

These laws were established in consideration of the fact that more and more criminals use the excuse that they were unconscious or cannot be remembered due to alcohol or drugs. Of course, some people may make such a claim because they really feel that way.

Such text is not required in the people's criminal law. Even if such a situation is suspected, the crime remains, and a thorough investigation can be conducted in the process of determining punishment. It is also not necessary in God's criminal law. If the unconscious state were induced with intent that results in a crime, there is no reason to state that it is not a crime.

However, let us recall that, historically, criminal law was developed in the perspective of the object of judgment.

Thus, this is a way to prevent the argument that narrowly interprets the text stating that intent is required in criminal law and that claims that because there was no intent while the criminal was committing the crime, though the criminal induced a state of unconsciousness themselves, it is not a crime.

6. MINORS

Some minors are not punished regardless of whether there is a crime. They are not punishable according to criminal law and are therefore special.

Criminal law has special provisions that do not punish minor children. Such crimes are distinguishable from other not-punishable grounds in that the criterion for a minor, who is not punishable, is age.

Setting the age limit for not-punishable minors is always a matter of concern, and the age limit is different depending on the time and place.

Let us consider whether the crime of a not-punishable minor is not a crime or whether it is a crime but not punishable.

The only criterion for not-punishable minors is age, and thus, there are variations. There are immature children, but there are young children who commit very cunning crimes. Such crimes enrage a great number of people.

There is no need to discuss whether an infant can be a criminal. However, there is a debate as to whether a child can become a criminal just before he/she exceeds the age limit, which is the criterion for not-punishable minors.

Thus, we cannot uniformly state whether a not-punishable minor can commit a crime. They are not punishable even if they commit crimes, so realistically, it is not easy to put forth enough effort to reveal the reality of a crime.

Some minors are not punished regardless of whether there is a crime. They are not punishable according to criminal law and therefore are special.

Some minors are not punishable in protecting people who are physically or mentally underdeveloped. Thus, we must not merely state that it is not a crime or it is not punishable when minors commit crimes. We need appropriate measures to respond to this. Not-punishable minors must be grouped based on their level of maturity, and appropriate measures for each group must exist. Further, because of differences in the level of maturity between individuals, there must also be a system to respond to this. Policy efforts regarding these issues are very important.

7. REDUCTION

Under God's criminal law, punishment is reduced in the same way that God shows generosity to God's creatures. Under the people's criminal law, however, punishment is decided after fierce deliberation about the criminal and crime.

Criminal law can impose heavier punishment or less punishment. If there is a reason to satisfy any condition set for the person who committed the crime, it is to control the amount of punishment according to the crime.

When a heavier punishment is meted, it is usually when a person who committed a crime and was punished for it commits the crime again or when the person has a habit of offending or special status. The heavy punishment for these people is not a big problem because it does not run counter to public sentiment.

However, those who enjoy academic discussions argue that punishing those who continue to commit crimes have no effect on making the criminal repent for their crimes. They claim that these people require treatment and are against punishing them.

This extreme divide is easy to understand and will generate academic interest. However, just because a law is from the old Bronze Age does not mean that it has no interest in reforming criminals.

Of course, as time has progressed, criminal laws have become more interested in criminals and have been working harder to make efforts and policies for their rehabilitation and reform, which is a desirable direction.

It has been the same in every period in time that one should be punished if one committed a crime and that one should be repentant and become a new person. This is the basic principle of criminal law and is at least fair. Interests in criminals and the results of research can be supplemented.

Criminal law began in the Neolithic Era, where human history began, and in the subsequent Bronze and Iron Ages, criminal law was only meant for revenge, as it is too simplistic, distorted, and not very persuasive. Those who make this argument lack sufficient consideration of our existence.

Contrary to increasing punishment, reduction in punishment leads to many questions. Punishment is increased for definite reasons—when a criminal who already received punishment commits a crime again or when they have a habit. Punishment may be decreased for definite reasons, such as a criminal attempting to or succeeding in compensating a victim, but it becomes problematic when the punishment is reduced because the criminal is regretful.

In most cases, the criminal will state that there was no intent or that he/she is regretful, hoping that it will be decided there is no crime or punishment, or punishment will be reduced. It is difficult to determine punishment according to certain criteria. The biggest problem is when punishment is reduced; it is based on a certain ratio, regardless of the reason.

For example, let us state that the punishment is reduced when the person who commits the crime is repentant; there is a special situation in the person's circumstances, or there is something to consider in the behavior around the crime. Here, if the decision to reduce the punishment is made, and punishment is given within the uniformly reduced scope set regardless of the reason or degree.

Though the criminal has committed a bad crime and though the crime has been acknowledged, sometimes when the punishment is reduced for various reasons, it results in the punishment being delayed; thus, the punishment is discarded under a set period or conditions.

Although a crime is committed, the punishment can be discarded or reduced if there is a good reason. As the punishment is reduced, the punishment can be delayed, or the criminal may be released and given freedom. It is important here that we conclude regarding what punishment to give after earnest consideration of the reason to discard or reduce the punishment for the criminal.

Under criminal laws with uniform reduction regulations, the decision is left to the system under the criminal law after deliberation on whether to reduce the punishment.

If the punishment is to be delayed and the criminal released, this must be the conclusion of the person determining the crime based on the criminal act in accordance with criminal law. It is not right that the criminal law itself makes the decision, nor that it is right that the conditions are met so that such a conclusion is made. The kind and amount of punishment to give should not be determined by the criminal law itself but by a person based on the criminal law.

Under God's criminal law, punishment is reduced in the same way as God shows generosity to God's creatures. Under the people's criminal law, however, punishment is decided after fierce deliberation about the criminal and crime.

Errors in the Conceptualization of the "Criminal Act" Based on the Principle of Essential Intent

ABSTRACT

Most criminal acts worldwide start with the intent for a crime to be committed, which is premised on the idea that intentionality must be revealed when determining that a criminal act has taken place. Because we are unable to know the intent of others, however, intent can cause errors within the criminal act; for example, revealing guilt based on the criminal act means making a rational judgement befitting of evidence and logic, rather than determining the existence of intent. If modern criminal investigation focuses on the type of crime, then it should be concerned with what punishment to allocate and to what degree. The present study examines errors that the principle of an essential intent of crime causes in the criminal act by focusing on crimes of robbery and rape. This study also contemplates what role intent should assume in the criminal act, and explores the perspective that a criminal act is based on the intellect, experience, and views of another person.

I. INTRODUCTION

In most criminal acts worldwide, the principle of essential intent to commit a crime[1] presumes that people are rational beings who follow and defend the laws created within the society to which they belong. Despite knowing that one should follow the law as a member of society, however, crimes are sometimes committed and laws are broken. This indicates that a criminal act answers the philosophical question of what kinds of beings we are.

It is here that this study asks one of the most important questions in the philosophy of law: "Are you able to know

---

[1] German criminal code article 15, French criminal code article 121-3, Austrian criminal code article 5, Swiss criminal code article 12, South Korean criminal code article 13, Chinese criminal code article 14, Japanese criminal code article 38

the intentionality of others?" This question straddles both spheres because it concerns our existence, which precedes the logic of law.

Philosophy was borne out of real-life problems, and the philosophy of law is no different, though there are limitations when applying philosophy to the law. This study explains these limitations by focusing on the topic of intent. In philosophy, intent can be viewed from different viewpoints; for example, whether the inquirer is speaking in the first person or not. This may, of course, include the limitations of human cognitive error. In discussing intent to commit a criminal act, which involves the law (i.e., crime and punishment), eventually such a discussion would end on the issue of what crime the subject committed and to what degree the subject, under the criminal act, should be punished. The agent who determines the crime and punishment based on the criminal act is not the individual who committed the crime, but is another person or persons. The individual who committed the crime does not decide his crime based on his own intent. Accordingly, the various meanings of intent discussed in philosophy, as well as their social implications, cannot be directly applied to the determination of a crime nor the punishment that follows as a result of the criminal act because a person is not able to know the intent of others. When discussing an intent to commit a criminal act, this inability to know the intent of others must be considered. Even if the idea or theory originates from a widely known philosopher who is viewed as an authority or expert, if the determination of intent was deduced from a purely philosophical perspective without considering its limitations in the criminal act, it cannot be applied objectively to the criminal act.[2]

The claim that no one knows the intent of others and, thus, intentionality is unnecessary for an act to become a crime first appeared in Jun-Hyung Park's book 'The Eyes of Criminal Law'. "We are not bettering our reason, but creating a good world with the reason we have."[3] This assertion can be difficult to accept, since it appears to be an obvious truth that requires no argument.

Since the modern age, philosophical discussions on human existence and cognition flowed seamlessly into theories on criminal acts, serving as the basis for the

---

[2] Jun-Hyung Park, Die augen des strafrechts, (Stuttgart: VERRAI, 2016), p.36

[3] Jun-Hyung Park, The Eyes of Criminal Law, (Ilsan: G-WORLD, 2015), p.12

principle of an essential intent of crime; however, this principle's penetration into the criminal act has caused massive errors.

The present study examines issues surrounding intent by presenting specific examples of errors caused by intent in the criminal act; specifically, that the need for intent in order for an act to become a crime is an error because we are unable to know the intent of others. As such, the criminal act itself, which would then reflect the principle of necessary intent, is an error. By maintaining that principle, but then amending it to reflect reality, contradicts the criminal law system. In other words, amending the principle to fit reality is a mission of the law, but establishing an unnecessary principle only to break it defies logic but also causes the serious issue of eroding trust in the law.

If I argue against the statement that "one cannot say that intent is necessary for there to be a crime," then the idea of an essential intent to commit a crime proclaims that the criminal act pursues even though we are unable to know the intent of others; as such, we must try our best to retain the principle of an essential intent of crime. Even if the principle of an essential intent of crime is feasible, and even if it can only demonstrate the ideals of the criminal act, then this discussion may not be necessary. However, it is not. The errors caused by intent's existence as an essential condition penetrate the criminal law system. The below sections examine detailed examples related to crimes of robbery and rape through the lens of the errors of essential intent.

II. CRIMES OF ROBBERY AND RAPE

This study chose crimes of robbery and rape to demonstrate the errors caused by intent in the criminal act because it using such specific examples can demonstrate this study's argument more so than using abstract and notional logic. Because there are numerous interpretations of what constitutes a criminal act in the world, this study focuses on societies that classify robbery and rape as criminal acts, though the study's findings do have implications for improving criminal law systems in societies that do not consider robbery and rape as criminal acts. The philosophy of law is never isolated from positive law.

Crimes of robbery and rape refer to an individual who commits both a robbery and a rape as part of a single criminal act. Crimes of robbery and rape in a criminal act that contains the principle of an essential intent are clearly distinct from crimes of rape and robbery, in which an individual who commits rape also commits robbery.[4] This is because the societies in which we focus this study consider sexual freedom to be more important than property and, as such, seeks to protect the sexual freedom of individuals more deeply.[5] The following parameters examine instances that become crimes of robbery and rape based on the intent of committing robbery and rape.

A. Cases in which the intent of rape arises in an individual who ends up committing rape only after committing robbery, without the initial intent of rape

B. Cases in which the intent of robbery arises in an individual who ends up committing robbery only after committing rape, without the initial intent of robbery

---

[4] This is a contrasting concept within crimes of robbery and rape, where an individual who commits robbery also commits rape. It refers to an individual committing robbery after committing rape as the crime of rape and robbery.

[5] Jun-Hyung Park, Die augen des strafrechts, (Stuttgart: VERRAI, 2016), p.20

C. Cases in which the initial intent was both robbery and rape, and rape is committed after the robbery

D. Cases in which the initial intent was both robbery and rape, and robbery is committed after rape

Case A is a typical scenario in which the intent of rape arises and is carried out after robbery is committed. On the surface, Case C appears to be similar to Case A without considering intent, and case D appears to be the same as case B. However, Cases C and D differ from cases A and B in that the intent of both robbery and rape existed from the onset. In Cases C and D, the intent of both robbery and rape co-existed, and only the sequence of the crimes differs. There may be dispute over whether Case D classifies as crimes of robbery and rape since robbery was committed after rape; as such, we must examine the necessity of the crimes of the robbery and rape to determine whether D can be classified in such a way.

Even if the crimes of the robbery and rape are not intended in any particular order, an individual who commits the crimes of robbery and rape is guilty of both, and handing out punishment based on this "pairing" does not create a vacuum in the criminal law system. The reason for grouping robbery and rape is to punish those crimes more heavily, rather than punish each act on its own.

Can punishing the crimes of robbery and rape together more heavily than each crime on its own faithfully achieve the legislative objective of protecting sexual freedom? The answer must consider whether the crimes of robbery and rape can be distinguished from their individual components in the criminal act where an intent must exist first for there to be a crime. Case A is typical of the crimes of robbery and rape, and Case B is typical of the crimes of rape and robbery. Cases C and D are instances that have the intent of both robbery and rape before the crime was committed, and appear outwardly similar to Cases A and B. What, then, are the differences between cases A and B? In Case A, robbery is committed with the intent of robbery (with no intent of rape); only after robbery is committed does the intent of rape arise and the act is carried out. In Case B, rape is committed with the intent of rape (with no intent of robbery), only after rape is committed does the intent of robbery arise and the act is carried out. Distinguishing between Cases A and B in this way means that each can be separated into a different type; however, being able to discern these two cases is yet another issue that will be discussed later. The above shows that the crimes of the robbery and rape are distinguishable from the crimes of the rape and robbery.

Next, we will examine whether harshly punishing the crimes of the robbery and rape is effective in protecting human sexual freedom. If it is clear that a person's sexual freedom is a more important value than a person's property, then punishing the crimes of the robbery and rape more harshly when paired together than crimes of rape and robbery on their own is convincing. Of course, the criminal acts of robbery and rape are often punished individually, but this does not create a vacuum in the criminal law system. Crimes of robbery and rape are more harshly punished to protect human sexual freedom when there is already a penal system in place for robbery and rape. If a rape was committed first, then the value of the person whose sexual freedom is being protected has already been damaged as a result of the crimes of the robbery and rape. The reason these two acts are treated in concert is because the victim is in a state of being overpowered by the assailant. Using this situation, the individual who committed robbery can also commit rape[6] ; as such, if only a robbery has been committed, then a strong warning is

---

[6] Jun-Hyung Park, Die augen des strafrechts, (Stuttgart: VERRAI, 2016), p.19

needed that condemns rape.[7] Cases C and D are considered as crimes of rape and robbery without considering the sequence of crimes because the intent of both robbery and rape already existed. This is because the crimes of the robbery and rape are understood to result in severe punishment for rape to an individual who had the intent of rape. A schematic of the relative severity of the crimes in cases A, B, and C may look like this: $b \langle a \langle c = d$. Cases C and D would be considered as more severe crimes[8] than Case A; however, without applying the crimes of robbery and rape, then Cases C and D would receive lighter punishments than Case A, creating a contradiction in the penal system.

The following are examples of the crimes of robbery and rape and serve to continue the discussion.

First are instances that include the criminal charge of both robbery and rape.

Charge: The crimes of robbery and rape

---

[7] Jun-Hyung Park, Die augen des strafrechts, (Stuttgart: VERRAI, 2016), p.23

[8] Cases A and C appear to be the same on the surface, but in the sense that both the intent of robbery and rape existed, would be more severe crimes than Case A.

Content: An individual who commits rape in the course of a robbery is put in prison for no less than 10 years.

This is the most typical form of a criminal act that includes the crimes of both robbery and rape. A particular law that includes robbery and rape was created to closely protect human sexual freedom.

Next is a case that does not, in particular, determine the criminal charge of robbery and rape, but raises the punishment for instances of rape in robbery.

Charge: The crime of robbery
Content: The individual who committed robbery is placed in prison for no less than 3 years. Individuals under this crime are placed in prison for no less than 10 years if they also commit rape.

III. ERRORS CAUSED BY CRIMINAL INTENT IN THE CRIMES OF ROBBERY AND RAPE

In most criminal acts, an intent is needed for there to be a crime; however, we are unable to know the intent of others. As such, an intent can cause errors in the criminal act. This section investigates this closely through crimes of robbery and rape.

Crimes of robbery and rape refer to an instance in which an individual who commits robbery also commits rape. Earlier, this study examined whether cases in which robbery was committed after rape fall into the category of crimes of robbery and rape. The determination to include these cases would be based on whether the intent of robbery existed prior to the rape, but if it did not exist prior to the rape, then these cases would not be included in that category. The problem, however, is that we are unable to know the intent(s) of the offender.

First, let us examine a case in detail where robbery was committed after rape. To be defined as a criminal act, there must be intent; accordingly, we should determine whether an act falls into the category of crimes of robbery and rape by clearly revealing intent. If there was no intent of robbery before committing rape, it does not fall into the crimes of robbery and rape; regardless, the person determining the crime is unable to know the intent of the offender but are only able to presume based on evidence and circumstance. Eventually, they must determine whether there was an intent of robbery, which will decide whether the offense falls into the crimes of robbery and rape. Of course, it is possible to claim that the best judgement on intent can be made by carefully examining evidence or circumstance when determining a crime based on the criminal act. If an intent is needed for there to be a crime, the meaning of intent within the criminal act is a choice between whether or not an intent existed when the crime was committed, and the potential for examination to approach the truth disappears. In this case, the essence of an intent to commit a criminal act is not the necessity for an act to become a crime, but as something that should be considered when allocating punishment.[9]

What would happen if the conclusion on intent, as based on the criminal act, was contrary to the truth?[10] Consider that there was an intent of both robbery and rape, and so after committing rape, that individual also commits robbery. This would fall into the crimes of robbery and rape. If the person making a judgement based on the criminal act, however, judges that it does not fall into the crimes of robbery and rape, since the intent of robbery could have appeared to arise only after rape was committed, then it is not crimes of robbery and rape. This conclusion could have been made according to the law rather than according to the facts concerning the crime.

This study focuses on the errors caused by intent in the criminal law system, where intent must exist for there to be a crime, even though the person determining the crime based on the criminal act is unable to know the intent of

---

[9] Jun-Hyung Park, Die augen des strafrechts, (Stuttgart: VERRAI, 2016), p.16

[10] One thing that must be noted is whether the person making a judgement based on the criminal act is making that judgement according to their own thoughts. This would be an issue of conscience, and this study does not discuss this; rather, this discussion focuses on the logic and rationale within the criminal law system.

others. This concerns the scope that a person is able to perceive in terms of determining a crime based on the criminal act, and is also a topic of philosophy as it relates to epistemology.

The perspective that determines a crime based on the criminal act is the intellect, experience, and views of another person. This point seems to have been overlooked when creating the premise that a criminal act must include intent for there to be a crime. Since we are unable to know the intent of others, the criminal act, as defined by our contemporaries, is fundamentally flawed. Discussions on whether intent must exist for there to be a crime is an issue of human nature that is unrelated to our abilities. The task at hand is not to make more diligent efforts to reveal an intent and gain a more meticulous logic, but rather to regain and reflect upon human nature. Revealing a crime does not reveal intent; rather, it only exposes the circumstances of the crime.[11] Recognizing our inability to know the intent of others must be the starting point for creating sensible laws.

---

[11] Jun-Hyung Park, Die augen des strafrechts, (Stuttgart: VERRAI, 2016), p.14

IV. SOLUTION

Japan recently amended their laws on criminal acts, wherein crimes of rape and robbery are now punished equally with crimes of robbery and rape.[12] Before the amendment, Japan viewed the crimes of rape and robbery separately, as rape and as robbery, but after amending the punishment for these crimes, the law now punishes them with the same severity as crimes of robbery and rape. This amendment is viewed as accommodating criticism that prior punishments differed based on the precedence relationship of the crimes.

The amendment of Japan's laws about robbery and rape has not only corrected the punishments to have equivalent

---

[12] Criminal act of Japan article 241

severity, but it also makes a distinction between both. As such, Japan's criminal act amended the crimes of robbery and rape because punishing these crimes with particular severity lost its meaning. The premise of this assumption, however, is that intent can be revealed based on the criminal act.[13] As examined earlier, the reason for harshly punishing the crimes of robbery and rape is because people are regarded as more important than property without relation to whether the crimes of robbery and rape are harshly punished. In this case, it cannot be determined that the reason for punishing the crimes of robbery and rape with particular severity has lost its meaning.

What inferences are possible under the premise that we are unable to know the intent of others even if we are able to ignore the significant principle of contemporary law.[14] In other words, intent must exist for there to be a crime; accordingly, we make a distinction between the crimes of robbery and rape and the crimes of rape and robbery,

---

[13] The criminal act is a standard that possesses legal force, not morals and ethics; accordingly, the criminal act that states there must be intent for there to be a crime presumes that intent can be revealed.

[14] Throwing away the principle of essential intent of crime changes the framework of the criminal act and means creating a new criminal act.

where punishment is provided heavily for the more severe crime of the two. Though it is clear that amending the criminal act to accommodate reality is an advisable task, the unity of the legal system cannot be ignored. Ideally, the various meanings and functions of the previous statutes for robbery and rape could be retained while amending the criminal act to fit reality without contradiction occurring in the legal system. This means that the difference in punishment should be proportionate to a priority on values that the criminal act seeks to protect in robbery crimes and rape crimes (i.e., it issues a strong warning to robbers intending to commit rape).

Crimes of robbery and rape under Japan's criminal act would not have been amended if the intent of robbery and rape could be accurately revealed. The case of Japan, where the crimes of rape and robbery were amended to punish the crimes with equal severity is a realistic method that maintains the principle of an essential intent of crime. This is a fundamental change that is urgently needed.

The following examines cases in which the crimes of robbery and rape have been amended in the criminal act. First are cases in which the principle of an essential intent of crime has been maintained, so we can consider methods that abolish the crimes of robbery and rape. This recognizes that we are unable to know the intent of others, and so even if the criminal act was created with the premise that intent can be revealed, since that is realistically an impossible task, this would be considered an accommodation that recognizes the reality that the intent cannot be revealed. This method would also abolish the crimes of robbery and rape, as there would be nothing to dispute. Then, the criminal act would ultimately have to move in the direction of abolishing the principle of an essential intent of crime.

Also consider the judgment that there is no need to punish the crimes of robbery and rape harsher than the crimes of rape and robbery. In this instance, a rape is a crime no worse than a robbery, or punishing robbery and rape more harshly than rape and robbery has no effect on preventing crime. Assuming that rape is a crime worse than robbery implies that human value is prioritized over property, which aligns with a shared human value and belief. If so, the key point in this case would be whether punishing the crimes of robbery and rape more severely than the crimes of rape and robbery has an effect on deterring robbers from committing rape. Under the criminal act, it is clear that designing a punishment that corresponds to the result of the crime can aid in crime prevention. Severe punishment for the crimes of robbery and rape can prevent robbers from moving on to also committing rape, and demonstrate that societies that uphold criminal laws are protecting human sexual freedom.

What about methods for punishing the crimes of rape and robbery equally with the crimes of robbery and rape? This raises the punishment for rape and robbery to the level of punishment established for robbery and rape, which reflects the reality that we are unable to know the intent of others while also maintaining the meaning[15] held by the crimes of robbery and rape. This method, however, cannot become a fundamental solution, as maintaining the principle of the essential intent of crime while also reflecting the reality that we are unable to know the intent of others is contradictory.

Next, how should the crimes of robbery and rape be

---

[15] The value of human sexual freedom is more important than property, and punishing crimes of robbery and rape harshly has an effect in deterring rape from being committed after a robbery is committed.

amended if the essential intent of crime is not needed in the criminal act? The cause of a common dispute in the crimes of robbery and rape is intent itself. If we could know another person's intent, we could distinguish between the crimes of robbery and rape and the crimes of rape and robbery, but if we are unable to know, then we cannot not make this distinction. Although it is clear that we are unable to know the intent of others, errors occur in the criminal act because an intent is needed for there to be a crime; as such, the issue of the crimes of robbery and rape and rape and robbery could be resolved more organically if intent was not considered essential to identifying that a crime has taken place. This does not stop simply at resolving the errors of the crimes of robbery and rape, but also changes the philosophy of the criminal act and moves the concern from what the crime is to what the punishment is and to what degree it should be given.

Below are some examples of what can occur in societies that consider the crimes of robbery and rape where an intent is needed for there to be a crime when robbery is committed after rape. Through this, the process through which an intent causes errors in the crimes of robbery and rape can be seen, and how this affects the criminal law system.

- A. The offender: From the beginning, the offender has the intent to commit both robbery and rape, and commits rape before committing robbery. According to the criminal act, a false assertion is made when the judgement states there was no intent of robbery before committing rape.

- B. The person determining the crime based on the criminal act: After contemplating the intent of the assailant based on evidence and circumstances, this person judges that the intent of robbery arose after committing rape and makes the conclusion that it does not fall into the category of crimes of robbery and rape.

- C. People witnessing this event: These people think that the punishment depends on which crime occurred first. They cannot accept that the crime changes based on whether the intent of robbery existed and are critical when the punishment changes based on the precedent relationship of the crime. They are more interested in to what degree the person should be punished than what crime it falls into.

D. A person intending to commit the crimes of robbery and rape: This person comes in contact with this event through planning a crime in which they will first commit rape and then commit robbery afterward.

The above examples demonstrate specifically the errors caused by intent. Because intent is needed for there to be a crime, errors occur as a result of the person determining the crime, who have to judge whether there was intent despite the person being unable to know the intent of others. This is an error that occurs throughout the criminal law system, not only limited to the crimes of the robbery and rape.

What would happen if an intent is not needed for there to be a crime? The important thing here is that no distinction is being made between the crimes of robbery and rape and the crimes of rape and robbery. Both are punished with equal severity.

A. The offender: This person has an intent to commit both robbery and rape from the beginning, and first commits rape and then commits robbery afterward. There is a false assertion, then, when receiving punishment according to the criminal act that there was no intent of robbery before committing rape.

B. The person determining the crime based on the criminal act: Based on evidence and circumstances, this person judges that the offender committed robbery after committing rape, and concludes that it is crimes of robbery and rape.

C. People witnessing this event: These people have no doubt that the individual who committed robbery and rape will be punished harshly.

D. A person intending to commit the crimes of robbery and rape: This person comes in contact with this event through the realization that he would be punished harshly if he were to commit robbery and rape together.

The above examples assume that intent is not needed for there to be a crime. It is possible to verify that the errors caused by an intent in determining crime have disappeared.

The distinction between the crimes of robbery and rape and the crimes of rape and robbery is an issue that occurs within the criminal act, where an intent is needed for there to be a crime. More than an issue inherent in any particular crime, this is an issue caused by the principle of an essential intent of crime. The criminal act presumes that we are able to clearly reveal another's intent; however, we are unable to know the intent of others, and the criminal act, which was designed under the premise that we can clearly reveal the intent, cannot bridge the gap between this ideal and reality, and will collapse.

If we contemplate the criminal act with the logic examined through the crimes of robbery and rape, a broader view of the errors caused by essential intent in the criminal act is clear. In the criminal act, crime is divided into a crime with intent and a crime due to mistakes. If dividing crimes in this way is done while understanding that intent in unknowable, this causes errors in not only the crimes of robbery and rape, but throughout the entire criminal law system. Continuing these discussions can help to create a foundation for improving the criminal act and can serve as the starting point of an authentic modern criminal act.

V. CONCLUSION

The contradictory principles of intent being needed for there to be a crime while understanding that knowing others' intent is an impossible task, the current criminal act can only determine a crime by using evidence and circumstance.[16] The principle of an essential intent of crime does not state that it must actually be that way, but proclaims that since humans are rational beings, they commit crimes despite knowing they should not do so. The criminal act, however, does not end in ethical proclamations; rather, it is the final bastion that must be strictly applied to crimes under the consent of members of society in order to maintain that society.

---

[16] Jun-Hyung Park, Die augen des strafrechts, (Stuttgart: VERRAI, 2016), p.16

If the principle of an essential intent of crime has a proper function in the criminal act, then there is no particular reason for eliminating it. This is a result of existing philosophies because it is a principle that anyone would agree with; however, the criminal act that states an intent must exist for there to be a crime presumes that we are able to clearly reveal the intent of others, and a criminal act designed in such a way causes errors in the established range of crimes. This, in turn, causes fatal errors in establishing punishments. Stating that an intent should not be necessary for there to be a crime is not synonymous with saying that an essential intent of crime is wrong, but rather that it is an ideal that is not achievable. Intent causes errors in the criminal act and also affects the entire criminal law system; as such, the principle of an essential intent of crime must be eliminated from the criminal act.

Granting the law an omniscient power does not guarantee authority. When we include a philosophy that everyone can accept, the law gains persuasiveness and can establish a truer, logical authority that can more effectively lead to order and harmony. This kind of law could grant us peace, and I hope that this study may be a signpost for the world to become that way.

JUN-HYUNG PARK

worldpeacefo@gmail.com
https://www.facebook.com/LawandPhilosophy
https://www.facebook.com/TheEyesofCriminalLaw

www.ingramcontent.com/pod-product-compliance
Lightning Source LLC
Chambersburg PA
CBHW031444210526
45464CB00005B/2329